Portrait of a Forest

Richard Kraus

Constable London

First published in Great Britain
in 1986 by
Constable and Company Limited
10 Orange Street
London WC2 H7EG

Hardback ISBN 0 09 467490 6

Paperback ISBN 0 09 4662207

Copyright Richard Kraus

Printed in England by
Hazell Watson & Viney Ltd.

Colour Reproductions by
Aero Offset Reproductions Ltd.

Portrait of a Forest is a photographic study of the New Forest in southern England. The book follows the acclaimed publication of *An English Forest* with seventy-five new pictures.

The photographs journey through the cycle of one year and are all taken at dawn. The collection of pictures speak for themselves without the need for text.